Electric Vehicle

Loaded with

Digital technology

Intelligence and conveniences

By

Andy Lee

Table of content

Preface

Since the birth of the first electric car in 1834 to the leading role of new energy vehicles at major international automotive exhibitions in 2011, new energy vehicles have gone through a journey of nearly 180 years. The car development process receives more attention than other types of cars, especially electric vehicles.

Entering the 21st century, the development of new energy vehicles has become a strategic focus for many countries and major car manufacturers in the world to address energy and environmental challenges.

China's new energy vehicles have a strong development momentum, which is developing rapidly in vehicle model matching, technology research and development, and new energy vehicle consumer markets, and has made breakthroughs in the fields of enterprises, technology, and markets.

Data shows that global electric vehicle sales reached 6.768 million units in 2021, an increase compared to previous year of 108.63 %; electric vehicle sales reached 10.522 million units in 2022, an increase of 55.47 %; and electric vehicles sales reached 13,500 million units in 2023, an increase of 35.47 %.

In term of engineering and technology perspective, new energy vehicles are becoming more sophisticated, their batteries are more powerful with longer cruising range, the vehicles are equipped infotainment with digital technology, adding intelligence and many other conveniences. Let's find out more...

The development history of electric vehicles

Electric vehicles are a new form of transportation that has attracted a lot of attention in recent years. They are not only environmentally friendly and energy saving, but also have the advantages of high efficiency and low noise. More and more people are starting to consider buying an electric vehicle.

Since the birth of the first electric car in 1834 to the leading role of new energy vehicles at major international automotive exhibitions in 2011, new energy vehicles have gone through a journey of nearly 180 years. After nearly two centuries of winding development, new energy vehicles have made unprecedented breakthroughs in type, technology, and market share. As subdivisions of electric vehicles, hybrid vehicles, pure electric vehicles and fuel cell vehicles dominate new energy vehicles. The car development process receives more attention than other types of cars. The century-old history of new energy vehicles can be divided into four stages: the birth of electric vehicles, the return of attention to electric vehicles, the development of other models such as hybrids, and the development of the pure electric vehicle market.

First stage: the birth of the electric vehicle. The first battery car invented by Englishman Thomas Davenport in 1834 was the world's earliest electric car. In the early 20th century, electric vehicles, internal combustion engine vehicles, and steam engine vehicles each accounted for a third of the US automobile market. In 1910, when internal combustion engine vehicles began to adopt large-scale assembly line production, their costs were greatly reduced, and electric vehicles because of their cruising range. Inadequate infrastructure such as short circuits and charging stations caused electric vehicles to withdraw from the market.

Second stage: electric vehicles are regaining attention. In the 1960s, the American government paid renewed attention to electric vehicles because of serious urban air pollution caused by tens of millions of cars. In the early 1970s, after the OPEC oil embargo crisis, gasoline prices soared and Western countries' interest in electric vehicles increased. The government has increased funding for electric vehicle research and development, and R&D bases have been established in various places, leading to the arrival of the second round of electric vehicle R&D climax.

Third stage: development of hybrid models and others. As people's awareness of sustainable development increases, more and more well-known companies are investing in the research and development of hybrid and pure electric vehicles. With the increasing number of hybrid vehicle models and the gradual increase in production and sales, many models have demonstrated good energy saving and environmental protection performance, which shows that the hybrid vehicle market has matured. Foreign car manufacturers designed the world's first hydrogen car in 1965, and China succeeded in making its first hydrogen car in 1980.

The fourth stage: market-oriented development of pure electric vehicles. In January 1994, the best electric car in the world at that time entered the testing phase. Four years later, the technically mature electric vehicle entered the trial operation stage. In 1996, the United States began producing and selling electric vehicles. This is the first electric car launched by a large manufacturing company using modern mass production methods. In November 2008, pure electric vehicles entered the new spring. Major auto market countries, including Europe, the United States and China, have included pure electric vehicles as the dominant direction of future development.

The development of new energy vehicles in developed countries

Regarding new energy vehicles, European and American countries began to pay attention to them in the mid-19th century and carried out relevant exploration. Hydrogen fuel products, biofuels and other technologies have also been launched. In the midst of the raging financial crisis, energy savings, environmental friendliness and new energy have become strategic choices for various countries. In terms of marketing, production and sales of new energy vehicles have entered a new stage of rapid development. In terms of policy planning, in recent years, the United States, Japan, Germany and other automotive industry powers have successively issued national plans to promote the development of the new energy vehicle industry, including hybrid vehicles. The Obama administration in the United States implemented the Green New Deal and plans to popularize 1 million plug-in hybrid electric vehicles by 2015. Japan regards the development of new energy vehicles as the core of the low-carbon revolution and plans to popularize 13.5 million vehicles next generation including hybrid vehicles by 2020. In November 2008, the German government proposed to popularize 1 million plug-in hybrid vehicles and pure electric vehicles in the next 10 years and stated that the implementation of the plan would mark Germany's entry into the era of energy vehicles. Of course, as the earliest and most advanced countries in the development of new energy vehicle technology, the United States, Japan, and Europe have become the propellers for the development of the new energy vehicle industry. Therefore, understanding the development status of the new energy vehicle industry through the United States, Japan and Europe is an unavoidable choice.

Electric Vehicles development in the U.S.

One of the founders of Tesla is Martin Eberhard, an engineer and car enthusiast from Silicon Valley. When he was looking for entrepreneurial projects, he found that the U.S. market lacked an electric car that was both environmentally friendly and fun to drive. He believes such a car could appeal to environmentally conscious and high-income consumers, such as those who own both a supercar and a Toyota Prius. So, he decided to build his own electric sports car.

On July 1, 2003, Eberhard co-founded Tesla Motors with his business partner Mark Tarpenning and named the company "Tesla Motors" to commemorate the physicist Nikola Tesla, a pioneer of alternating current and radio transmission. They began looking for the investment and materials needed for an efficient electric sports car.

They soon found an electric car company called AC Propulsion, which had produced an electric sports car called the T-Zero, which used thousands of laptop lithium batteries as power and was capable of covering a distance of 480 kilometers of cruising range. Eberhard hoped to learn from the technology of this car and received the support of the CEO of AC Propulsion.

However, they also need a suitable partner to provide capital and management experience. At this time, they met Elon Musk, a successful entrepreneur and investor who had founded companies such as PayPal and SpaceX. Musk was interested in Eberhard's idea and invested $6.3 million in Tesla in February 2004, becoming the company's first investor and chairman.

Tesla's first product

Tesla began developing their first product, the Tesla Roadster, a pure electric sports car based on the British Lotus Elise. The car uses motors and control systems provided by AC Propulsion, as well as battery packs and chassis designed by Tesla itself. It has amazing performance, accelerating from 0 to 60 miles per hour in just 3.7 seconds, reaching a top speed of 201 kilometers per hour, and a cruising range of 394 kilometers.

However, the development process of Roadster was not smooth. It encountered many technical difficulties and cost issues. One of the biggest challenges is how to design a transmission with high performance, high efficiency, high safety, and low cost. Tesla has tried a variety of solutions, but they have all failed. In the end, Tesla decided to abandon the multi-stage gearbox and use a single-stage gearbox. Although it sacrificed some acceleration performance, it also reduced complexity and cost.

Another problem is that the production cost of the Roadster far exceeded expectations, causing Tesla to have to increase the selling price from the original $100,000 to $110,000. This caused dissatisfaction and cancellations from some pre-order customers. Tesla is also facing a severe cash shortage and has had to lay off employees and seek more financing.

Tesla's breakthrough

In February 2008, Tesla finally began delivering the first batch of Roadsters, with the initial seven vehicles offered as a "Founders Series" to Musk and other backers, including Google's Larry Page and Sergey B. Lin, eBay's Jeff Skoll, and others. Subsequently, Tesla gradually expanded the sales scope of Roadster to include markets such as Europe, Asia, and Australia. From 2008 to 2012, Tesla sold more than 2,250 Roadsters in 31 countries.

At the same time, Tesla has also begun to provide electric vehicle parts and technical services to other car companies. In 2008, Tesla reached a cooperation agreement with Daimler to provide battery packs and motors for its Smart brand. Daimler also invested $70 million to acquire a 10% stake in Tesla. In 2009, Tesla signed a cooperation agreement with Toyota to provide it with battery packs and electric engines, and purchased a factory in Fremont, California, from Toyota to produce its next-generation products.

On June 29, 2009, Tesla successfully listed on Nasdaq and became the first pure electric vehicle manufacturer listed in the United States. The IPO price was US$17, and net proceeds were US$184 million. On the opening day, Tesla's stock price rose 40.53% to close at $23.89. The listing brought more money and reputation to Tesla.

Tesla's Transformation

After the successful launch of Roadster, Tesla was not satisfied with being a niche electric sports car manufacturer but began to transform into an electric car manufacturer targeting a wider range of consumers. It began to develop more practical, economical, and smart electric vehicle products and build its own brand image and sales channels.

On June 22, 2012, Tesla released its second product-Tesla Model S, a full-size luxury electric sedan. This car has more space, higher cruising range, stronger performance, more innovative features, and a lower price. It uses an all-aluminum alloy body, a 17-inch touch screen, liftable air suspension, super charging station and other technologies. It also has a self-developed automatic driving system (Autopilot), which can realize automatic lane changing, automatic parking, automatic summoning, and other functions.

Model S has received widespread praise and recognition since its launch. It has received awards including Automobile Magazine. Car of the Year, the Society of Automotive Engineers' Car of the Year, and many other awards. It has also set many records, such as the fastest four-door sedan, the safest car, the highest consumer satisfaction, etc.

On September 29, 2015, Tesla released its third product-Tesla Model X, a full-size luxury electric SUV. This car continues the excellent performance and innovative design of Model S, while adding more functions and features, such as falcon-wing rear doors, panoramic windshield, bio-defense mode, optional third-row seats, etc. It is also the first Tesla vehicle to have self-driving hardware and can gain more self-driving features through software upgrades.

On March 31, 2016, Tesla released its fourth product-Tesla Model 3, a mid-size electric sedan. This car is a key product for Tesla to realize the third phase of its "secret plan", which aims to popularize electric vehicles to a wider market and consumers. It has the same performance and technology as the Model S and Model X, but the price is only about half of the first two, starting at $35,000. It is also the first time Tesla has adopted standardization and mass production to reduce costs and improve efficiency.

Model 3 sparked an unprecedented booking boom upon its release, with more than 180,000 orders received in just 24 hours, setting the largest booking record in automotive history. As of the end of 2018, Model 3 has become the best-selling luxury sedan in the United States and has achieved impressive sales and reputation worldwide.

Tesla's future

After ten years of development, Tesla has grown from a niche electric sports car manufacturer to a world-leading electric vehicle and energy company. It not only produces four excellent electric vehicle products, but also establishes its own super charging station network, energy storage system, solar roof, and other businesses. It also continues to carry out technological innovation and improvement, such as launching more advanced autonomous driving systems, more efficient battery technology, and smarter software platforms.

Tesla also has more ambitious visions and plans, such as launching more types and price ranges of electric vehicle products, such as the upcoming Tesla Model Y (a compact electric SUV), Tesla Semi (an electric truck), Tesla Roadster 2.0 (a super electric sports car), etc.; such as achieving global super charging station coverage and solar roof installation; such as realizing fully autonomous driving and driverless taxi services; such as exploring areas such as Mars colonization and hyperloop.

In short, Tesla is a company that constantly challenges itself, constantly breaks through limits, and constantly changes the world. It spent a decade proving that electric cars were not only possible, but better. It uses its actions to achieve its mission: to accelerate the world's transition to sustainable energy.

Folding the development of China's new energy vehicle industry

China's journey to becoming the most important player in the EV industry started in the early 2000s, when Chinese realized it would never overtake the U.S, Germany, and Japan legacy automakers on internal combustion engines. So, China decided to pivot to the most extreme option left. If China could produce the best cars in the world that were 100% powered by batteries at the time, the risk was extremely high, but China had extra motivation. First the EV vehicle provided China a chance to truly become a dominant player in the overly saturated automobile industry. Second, by investing in EV vehicles China could solve some of the country's other problems reducing severe air pollution and reducing its reliance on imported oil. Also, China already has some structural advantages, whereas EV manufacturing involves different technologies. This still requires the cooperation of the existing automotive supply chain, and China has a relatively complete supply chain, and the manufacturing capacity and talent support. Its gasoline car factories can also be transferred to support the emerging electric vehicle industry. Therefore, the Chinese government took measures to invest in related technologies as early as 2001, when electric vehicle technology was listed as a priority scientific research project in China's five-year plan.

China's new energy vehicles have strong development momentum. They are developing rapidly in vehicle model matching, technology research and development and the new energy vehicle consumer market, and have made breakthroughs in the fields of enterprise, technology, and market.

Enterprise development

China's local vehicle manufacturers have two models for developing new energy vehicles. One is to find a way only through the resources they own. Major car companies have been researching and developing new energy vehicles for a long time, and the large-scale launch of concept cars and trial operations only appeared after the promulgation of the Plan in 2009. All car manufacturers have invested in the battle for new energy vehicles. The governments of major automobile industry provinces such as Jilin, Anhui, Guangdong, and Hunan have also been staking out land and issued policies to encourage local large-scale automobile companies to establish new energy vehicle bases in an attempt to gain strong support from policies. At present, nearly a hundred automobile companies across the country have invested in the research and development of new energy vehicles. Not only automobile manufacturers, but also energy suppliers, supporting facility construction companies and technology research and development companies are also involved in the upsurge of new energy vehicles supporting construction. Led by the State-owned Assets Supervision and Administration Commission and established by central enterprises, the New Energy Vehicle Central Enterprise Alliance was established on August 18, 2010. The involvement of major groups indicates that the technical standards will be more unified, and the concentration of enterprises will be further increased.

Current technology development

China has implemented new energy vehicle technology planning starting in early 2000. Over the decade, China has invested 204 billion yuan in scientific research funds to implement the plan, electric vehicle science and technology projects, energy conservation, and energy vehicle projects. In the past 10 years, more than 500 related topics have been established, and independent research and development of electric vehicles and other energy-saving new energy vehicles have been continuously encouraged, forming three technical lines with pure electric vehicles, gasoline-electric hybrids, and fuel cells. General technology electric vehicle research and development patterns: multi-energy powertrain, control systems, drive motors and their control systems, and power batteries and their management systems. After decades in scientific and technological research, China has made significant progress in the field of new energy vehicles. The company has established an electric vehicle power system, technology platform and vehicle integration technology with independent intellectual property rights and developed a series of large-scale application products. The overall level is at the forefront of international.

While promoting the development of electric vehicle research and development, China is also actively promoting the talent, patent, standard strategy, striving to gain a say in future competition. In the implementation of the science and technology plan alone, 2,881 patents have been applied for, including 1,635 special invention projects, and 42 national and industry standards for electric vehicles have been promulgated.

However, in terms of new energy technology, China and foreign countries are not yet on the same starting line. In terms of key components such as automotive lithium batteries, drive motors, and power control systems, there is still a gap between China and developed countries.

Market development

China's traditional automobile industry market is in good condition, reflected in the rapid growth of automobile production and sales. The China Association of Automobile Manufacturers released the 2010 domestic automobile production and sales statistics. In 2010, China's automobile production and sales exceeded 18 million units, higher than the 13 million units in 2009. The year-on-year growth was the highest in history. Passenger car production and sales exceeded 10 million units for the second time. Commercial vehicles generally performed well. The rapid development of the automobile industry in 2010 made China continue to be the world's largest automobile producer and consumer. The new energy vehicle market is slowly starting up. As of January 2011, a total of 330,000 new energy vehicles have been sold in China, 80% of which are hybrid electric vehicles. At the same time, the cumulative sales of foreign new energy vehicles in China are 160,000. In addition, new energy vehicles developed by some automobile companies have been successively launched in pilot cities for promotion.

The rise of electric vehicles in China

In 2001, China decided to provide funding for research and development projects for battery-powered vehicles, as well as fuel cells and hybrid vehicles. But the real turning point came in 2008, when Mr. Wan Gang, a former automotive engineer, became China's Minister of Science and Technology, and he was also a fan of Tesla cars. Under the leadership of Mr. Wan Gang, China's Ministry of Science and Technology introduced subsidies for the purchase of new energy vehicles for the first time. Electric vehicles are also joining the ranks of taxis and government procurement vehicles. Electric vehicles are gradually taking shape in China, and the entire supply chain of the electric vehicle industry in China has also been formed. The country has benefited from Chinese industrial technology, battery production and even mineral refining.

Some relatively established Chinese automakers, such as BYD, which started out producing lithium batteries, have been able to expand their strengths in the electric vehicle space, while startups such as Leapmotor and Nio have also quickly emerged. The Chinese government has supported every step taken by domestic companies. Providing assistance for development, and this assistance is not limited to subsidies and government procurement. Government uses cheap capital or shares to give these young companies a boost.

There is only one problem remaining in China's developing electric car market, namely that the quality of domestic cars at that time is not good enough to enter the international market and cannot compete with luxury electric car brands such as Tesla. But this would soon change, when China allowed Tesla to build a factory in Shanghai, Tesla brought new competition to the Chinese electric vehicle market, and more importantly, it raised the bar for Chinese suppliers. These suppliers produce electric vehicles components according to the specifications provided by Tesla. After accessories and spare parts, which can also provide components of similar quality to Chinese car manufacturers. As if overnight, domestic Chinese cars suddenly met all standards, their production periods were shorter, prices were more competitive, and the quality was still very good, sometimes even higher than Western competitors. China's electric vehicle market expanded rapidly in 2021, with sales increasing 170% from the previous year to around 3 million vehicles. That year, almost half of the world's electric vehicle sales came from China. Among them, BYD is the sales champion, and Tesla only ranks third. The era of electric vehicles has officially begun, and for the first time, Chinese automakers are standing center stage, suddenly becoming a leading international electric car manufacturer with highly competitive capabilities. At that time, Western car manufacturers didn't seem to feel the crisis.

In 2022, it will be an important year for China's new energy vehicle transformation, and it will also be an extraordinary year for China's electric vehicles. BYD's sales managed to overthrow and surpass global new energy leader Tesla.

The future is quite promising, whether China can develop from a big country with new energy vehicles to a strong automobile country is expected to change. In recent years, with the continuous increase in global environmental protection awareness, the market demand for electric vehicles has gradually become more attractive.

As the world's largest car market, China is also the world's largest car producer. One of the countries with the fastest growing new energy vehicle market in the world. In 2022 the production of new energy vehicles will reach 3 million in just one year, more than any other country. Currently, the number of new energy vehicles in China has reached 17 million, and by the end of 2023, new energy vehicles will reach 20 million. It has become a consensus that competition in the automotive market is increasingly fierce, and the new energy automotive market is undergoing a shake-up. Recently, Wang Chuanfu, chairman of BYD, said at the general meeting of shareholders that unlike previous years (2022) when the supply of new energy vehicles was limited, this year 2023 the market has entered an era of oversupply, and the industry will see the survival of the fittest. In the next 3 to 5 years, the new energy vehicle industry will experience major changes, and the slower the market, the more unpredictable and difficult it will be to judge. On July 5, 2023, among 16 new energy automakers, including Tesla, signed an agreement to stop the bloody price war, so many foreign media reported relatedly, saying that in the future, the industry should stop fighting this kind of thing price war, and everyone must work together to improve quality and technology.

On the other hand, large manufacturers such as Volkswagen, Toyota and Honda are at least better than Chinese automakers and Tesla in terms of scale. Then this scale advantage will also be imitated by electric vehicles in the market? That's not necessarily the case. What's really missing is infotainment, and car karaoke. Likewise, traditional car manufacturers often encounter obstacles in the electric vehicle sector, such as battery manufacturing costs and of course software development. It is known that these large manufacturers may have the best automotive engineers, but they are not necessarily good at programming. This weakness was fully revealed when Volkswagen launched the ID3 series electric vehicle in 2021. It was discovered that the operating system was buggy and slow. Current car owners still have to go to the dealer to update the system. In contrast, Chinese car companies have implemented remote system updates. The ID3 problem has not escaped the attention of Chinese car reviewers. Other foreign car manufacturers have also experienced this, with many problems. Mercedes-Benz and Toyota have both had to recall products in China due to software problems. Tesla even carried out a massive car recall due to software problems. Even if these shortcomings are put aside, compared to Chinese competitors, most of which have foreign brands, there are still a few obstacles in developing electric vehicles. They don't have many interesting gimmicks, like selfie cameras or in-car karaoke. For Volkswagen executives, ignoring these software issues and misreading the needs of the Chinese market was just their initial mistake.

Although admitting errors is the first step to improvement, major car manufacturers including Volkswagen, Toyota and Honda are still not free from software problems. In addition, these foreign brand electric vehicles are gradually losing their appeal in the Chinese market in terms of price, reliability, and performance. Especially in the context of the Chinese consumer market which is increasingly influenced by nationalist tendencies.

What should the Western automakers do? It can only lower prices! In recent months, Volkswagen and Tesla cars have reduced prices significantly in China. This is not a strategy; it is a helpless move. The Chinese market is already highly saturated, and major automakers are doing their best to maintain their market share. In August 2023, Volkswagen's sales did soar due to price reductions, but because consumers' purchasing interest in internal combustion engine vehicles was getting lower, and Volkswagen's overall share of the Chinese car market continued to decline. After controlling around 15% of the Chinese market for many years, Volkswagen's market share falls to 11.4% in 2022. For Japanese automotive giants, such as: Toyota and Honda, the situation is even worse, with their market share falling by almost 6% per year and continuing to decline. At the same time, in the first half of 2023, BYD replaced Volkswagen as the largest car brand in China. It could be said that these traditional Western cars have learned a painful lesson in China this time. Complacency won't work! Don't underestimate the Chinese government's industrial policies.

Volkswagen also took swift action to correct its mistakes, such as by investing in China's technology industry. In recent months, Volkswagen first announced a joint venture with Chinese software development company ThunderSoft, and then invested in Xpeng Motors. The two parties will jointly develop two electric models that are scheduled to be launched in 2026. But the problem is that they have lost valuable time. And now, the other shoe is about to drop. The saturation of the Chinese domestic market has forced Chinese automakers to turn their attention to international markets. If traditional Western car brands are already having a hard time in the Chinese market, then in the global market, they will face even more difficult days. It will start from the Munich International Auto Show 2023. It can be seen that BYD is one of the most famous exhibitors. It has launched five new models for the European market. Chinese automakers believe that not only Chinese people, but consumers around the world need more digitally connected cars.

New energy vehicles are an important industrial sector, providing many job opportunities and are a barometer of a country's industrial progress. It would be a shame if it was just ignored.

The Electric Vehicles Market

Entering the 21st century, the development of electric vehicles has become a strategic focus for many countries and major automobile manufacturers in the world to respond to energy and environmental challenges. The world's new energy automobile industry has entered a period of comprehensive upgrading. Global carbon emission reduction actions are in-depth, and electrification in the transportation field has driven a rapid increase in the number of new energy vehicles. Data shows that global electric vehicle sales reached 6.768 million units in 2021, a year-on-year increase of 108.63%; in 2022, sales reached 10.522 million units, a year-on-year increase of 55.47%; in 2023 sales reached 13.337 million units, a year-on-year increase of 35.47%. Cumulative global sales of new energy vehicles are approximately 37.7 million units, with China accounting for approximately 60%.

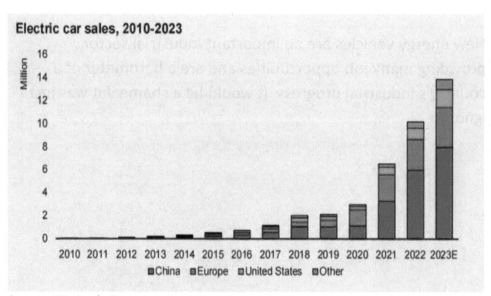

Electric car sales, 2010-2023

Source: IEA Analysis

Top 10 Global Electric Vehicles Sales by companies in 2023

Ranking	Manufacturers	Sales volume
1	BYD - China	3,024,417
2	Tesla - USA	1,810,000
3	Stellantis - Europe	1,527,090
4	SAIC-GM-Wuling – China	1,403,066
5	Volkswagen - Germany	531,500
6	Geely - China	487,461
7	GAC-Aian - China	480,003
8	Ideal motor – China	376,030
9	Great Wall – China	261,546
10	Modern Group - South Korea	257,000

Note: Include EV, PHEV, FCV. Source: Writer Analysis

At present, China's new energy vehicle market is dominated by independent brands, and the sales of Chinese brand-new energy passenger vehicles account for a high proportion of the total sales of new energy passenger vehicles. According to data from the China Association of Automobile Manufacturers, in 2023, the sales of the top ten enterprise groups in new energy vehicle sales will account for 82.2% of total new energy vehicle sales. Among them, BYD Auto has become the sales volume of new energy vehicles ranks first, with a market share of 33.6%; SAIC-GM-Wuling rank second and Tesla rank third with market shares of 15.5% and 10.5% respectively. The top ten companies are not yet stable.

In 2023, Electric Vehicle sales in China, as follow:

Ranking	Manufacturers	Volume (unit)	Market Share
1	BYD	3,024,417	33.6 %
2	SAIC-GM-Wuling	1,403,066	15.5 %
3	Tesla (Shanghai)	947,000	10.5 %
4	Geely	487,461	5.4 %
5	GAC-Aian	480,003	5.3 %
6	Ideal Motor	378,030	4.2 %
7	Great Wall	261,546	2.9 %
8	Nio	160,038	1.7 %
9	Li Auto	144,155	1.6 %
10	Xiaopeng	141,601	1.5 %

Source: China Association of Automobile Manufacturers

China Electric Vehicles market share in 2023

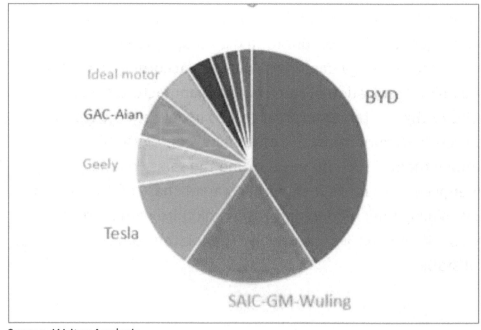

Source: Writer Analysis

Under the dual effects of policy and market, China's new energy vehicle industry will enter a period of comprehensive market expansion in 2023, with penetration rates increasing rapidly. In terms of scale, China has become the world's largest new energy vehicle market, with production and sales ranking first in the world for eight consecutive years. According to statistics, China's new energy vehicle sales will be 9.0 million units in 2023, a year-on-year increase of 35.9%, and the penetration rate will reach 25.6%. The New Energy Vehicles will be completed ahead of schedule. The phased goals for 2025 set in the Industrial Development Plan (2021-2035) have entered an explosive period of scale expansion and an expansion period of comprehensive marketization.

There are more than 35 automakers in China, among them: BYD (比亚迪), Saic-GM-Wuling (上汽通用五菱), Geely (吉利), GAC-Aian (广汽埃安), Idealmotor (理想), Great wall (长城), Nio (蔚来), Xiaopeng (小鹏), etc.

China exports Electric Vehicles

China's auto exports are expected to maintain growth momentum throughout the year, making China the world's largest auto exporter in 2023.

Supported by product and technological advantages, and driven by Chinese automakers' increased investment in channels, R&D, and product localization, electric vehicles are expected to continue to be the core driver of China's auto export growth.

According to Canalys forecasts, by 2023, China's automobile exports will reach 5.26 million units, of which electric vehicles will account for 40.2%, reaching 2.114 million units.

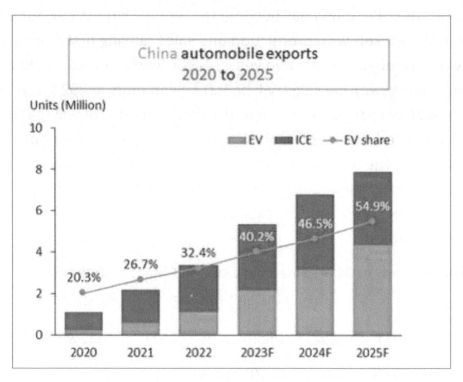

Electric vehicles from Chinese brands are performing better, especially in markets in Southeast Asia, the Middle East and Africa. Here, demand for the transition to electric vehicles is growing, with Chinese brands' market shares reaching 71% and 63% respectively. BYD is the best-selling electric vehicle brand in Southeast Asia, with a 39.8% share of the region's electric vehicle market. It is worth noting that BYD is the only brand in the electric vehicle market with a market share of more than 10%.

Although the penetration rate of electric vehicles in Latin America is relatively low, Chinese brands have accumulated channel and brand influence before promoting electric vehicle products, achieving 58% of the Latin American electric vehicle market share.

Considering export volume, product mix and competitiveness in some regional electric vehicle markets, China's automobile industry is about to complete the first step of its globalization strategy, from 'going out'. It is gradually transitioning to the 'entry' stage, which is a global journey that involves balancing advanced connectivity technologies with local user preferences, enhancing local consumer trust, and building brand strength and brand image is critical.

China's Electric Vehicles export in 2023

Rank	Manufacturers	Volume (unit)	Market share
1	Saic-GM-Wuling	302,000	17.7 %
2	Tesla	290,000	16.7 %
3	Geely	264,000	12.9 %
4	GAC-Aian	251, 000	12.8 %
5	BYD	243,000	11.4 %
6	Chang'an	170,000	10.8 %
7	JAC Group	90,000	6.5 %
8	Chery Automobile	80,000	5.6 %
9	Dongfeng	35,000	2.1 %
10	Others	33,000	2.9 %

Source: Writer Analysis

There are about 35 brands exporting electric vehicles from China. However, the top five brands accounted for 71.5 % of the market share in the year of 2023. Tesla is the only automaker among the top five exporters that is not a local Chinese car brand. However, most overseas markets are still in the early stages of electric vehicle transformation, and consumer demands are constantly changing. We expect even greater growth.

Data from the China Custom Authority shows that auto companies will export 5.221 million vehicles in 2023, a year-on-year increase of 57.4 %. Exports of new energy vehicles will reach 177,300,000 units, increasing 67.1 % year-on-year. China's domestic car sales in the same period were 30.01 million vehicles. Domestic and export car demand is increasing rapidly, this is because the industrial structure itself is complete and production capacity is strong. Besides that, China's automotive consumer market is very strong, and the products it produces have a very strong influence on a global scale, with very competitive prices. Behind the boom in Chinese car exports is a good business environment between importing and exporting countries, good appeal, performance and quality, coupled with digital connections, network intelligence and conveniences.

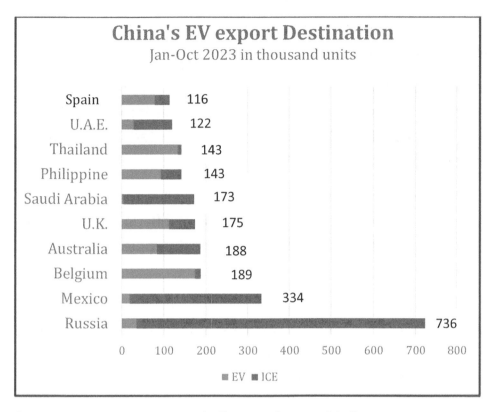

China's EV export Destination
Jan-Oct 2023 in thousand units

Spain	116
U.A.E.	122
Thailand	143
Philippine	143
Saudi Arabia	173
U.K.	175
Australia	188
Belgium	189
Mexico	334
Russia	736

■ EV ■ ICE

These countries are spread all over the world, from Western Europe to Southeast Asia, and from the Middle East to Latin America.

The reason for Russia is the most special. Previously, Russia's automobile manufacturing industry has always relied on Western investment, parts supply and partnerships. Affected by the Russia-Ukraine conflict, a large number of multinational car companies stopped exporting to Russia, supplying spare parts and stopped producing cars in Russia. In March 2023, Avtovaz, Russia's largest automobile manufacturer, announced that due to a shortage of parts, the factory would open early and postpone the summer vacation. Affected by this, Russia's automobile consumption has completely entered the sales market, and vehicle prices have generally increased.

In this context, Chinese car companies that can provide stable supplies have been benefited. In 2022, Russia imported 117,000 passenger cars from China and in 2023 imported 730,000 units, increasing 5-fold.

For Mexico, even though it neighbors the USA, the price of American cars feels expensive, because of inflation. Meanwhile, Chinese cars are more affordable for most people who do not have high incomes.

China's automobile exports are currently encountering a problem due to the lack of sufficient automobile transportation vehicles. Chinese automobile manufacturers have difficulty transporting the cars they produce, and China needs more ro-ro ships.

From 2019 to 2022, China's automobile exports volume increased sixfold, but freight rates increased by 800%. They use a 40" container, which can accommodate 4 cars, or with a modification container frame, which can accommodate more cars in total.

There are more than 700 ro-ro ships in the world, but less than 100 of them are operated by Chinese companies. The China Shipbuilding Industry reported in the summer of 2023 that only about ten ships were suitable for ocean shipping. According to research, until 2026 Chinese shipyards will build about 200 ro-ro ships, 76 of which will be built for Chinese customers. One large ro-ro ship can accommodate 7,000-9,000 cars.

In addition, due to the large number of cars exported from China, a strange phenomenon has emerged. Large areas of some Chinese ports have been converted into parking lots for new cars, waiting for export.

Chinese electric vehicles have a huge impact to Western automakers, with the average cost of an electric vehicle in China being less than half that of an electric vehicle in the United States or European Union, leading to a widening price gap. In China, anyone can afford an electric car, it is cheaper than internal combustion engine car.

China has incomparable advantages in manufacturing, as follow:
Complete industrial chain
Complete industrial system
Many well-trained skilled workers
Many capable engineers
Huge consumer market
World class infrastructure
Stable political environment
The government supports business development. This advantage is also reflected in the industrial cluster, electric power, petrochemical, smelting, heavy machinery, etc. This upstream industry, which benefits the downstream manufacturing industry, with controlled prices, is the foundation of the national economy.

Average retail price of electric vehicles in 2023 (USD)

Regions	Chinese Brand	Non-Chinese Brand
China	$ 25,947	$ 78,055
India	$ 27.714	$ 57,994
Japan	$ 29,639	$ 67,236
South East Asia	$ 33,613	$ 123,807
Australia / New Zealand	$ 37,434	$ 78,055
Turkey	$ 46,834	$ 102,814
Latin America	$ 49,178	$ 106,110
Europe	$ 51,516	$ 71,784
Israel	$ 60.153	$ 124.498
USA / Canada	–	$ 68,588
South Korea	–	$ 78,874
South Africa	–	$ 100.820

Source: Jato Dynamics

Judging from the table above, electric vehicles from European and American brands are generally priced higher, while Chinese electric vehicles sold in these countries/regions are much cheaper. The reason is China's manufacturing advantage and cheaper battery chemistry helps reduce the cost of electric vehicles. In addition, lower energy costs from Russia, due to sanction from the West.

Western media also claim that the Chinese government provides large subsidies for electric vehicles. Although the United States and European countries also provide tax incentives. In fact, the implementation of subsidy measures is also a common international rule. China's approach has been more successful, it has passed the subsidy stage and with the orderly withdrawal of state subsidies, China's subsidies for new energy vehicles have already been terminated at the end of 2022. Currently the competitiveness of China's Electric Vehicles is based on China manufacturing advantage, innovation in additional intelligence (self-parking without driver, stopping if lane is interrupted), digitally connected (functions as a smartphone or iPad with a larger screen) and many conveniences (projection screen, safety box with passcode, small box cooler).

To vigorously develop the new energy vehicle industry, every country will adopt various incentives. In terms of subsidy strength, the U.S. tax credit of US$ 7,500 is quite a lot. In order to increase the market share of new energy vehicles, the Japanese government will double subsidies to consumers who purchase new energy vehicles starting in the spring of 2022, up to a maximum of 2.5 million yen (approximately US $ 17,600).

Interesting story. In 2023, the largest publishing house in Japan is called BP. They bought a Chinese BYD Seal car. They completely disassembled it, and used a camera to photograph it from beginning to end, including the chassis, battery, all dismantled. After dis-assembling, a book was released with detailed breakdown diagrams. This book is very expensive in Japan, selling for 880,000 yen (US $ 6,200). If you want to add some videos and other explanations, it is more expensive at 1.32

million yen (US $ 9,300). The Japanese hope to understand Chinese cars, which have very powerful technology inside.

The United States and the European Union have both engaged in trade protectionism, of course it is disadvantageous for China to export cars. However, looking at it from another perspective, this move by the United States and the European Union is tantamount to bringing their own automobile industries to self-destruction, only competition can bring progress. The Chinese government dared to allow Tesla to set up factories in China in 2019, and dared to let Tesla's electric cars invade, the Chinese government was not worried about this or that at the time.

If the United States and European Union continue to engage in trade protection, at least one thing is certain. The United States and European Union can only close the door and sell their own cars domestically. At the most, they will completely lose their competitiveness, and world markets will be dominated by Chinese cars. In another word, the United States and European Union are handing over vast overseas markets to China. Its impact goes beyond that, Chinese industries will reverse the past impression of cheap products to overseas consumers. China will replace the image of high-end products in the United States, European Union, and Japan, and establish a new high-end brand.

What should the Western countries do when their high-end industries are increasingly impacted by China? In fact, there is really no good way, because this is the law of competition. The only way is to join and integrate into the Chinese economic circle, such as: Tesla, Volkswagen and others.

The technology of electric vehicles

As the world pays more and more attention to environmental issues, new energy vehicles, as an environmentally friendly and energy-saving mode of travel, have attracted more and more people's attention. The core technology of new energy vehicles is an important support for their efficient and reliable operation. The following will focus on the core technologies and beyond of new energy vehicles, as follows:

1. Battery technology

The battery technology of new energy vehicles is one of its most basic core technologies. The performance and quality of the battery are not only related to the cruising range and service life of the car, but also directly related to the safety of the vehicle. Currently, lithium-ion batteries are the most important battery type for new energy vehicles. Lithium-ion batteries have high energy density, long life, and good safety, and have become the mainstream of new energy vehicle battery technology.

Lithium metal anode battery technology: The emergence of this technology has greatly improved the charging speed and cycle life of the battery. Lithium metal negative electrodes allow for faster charging and reduce the risk of battery swelling and rupture. The other, Solid-state battery technology, which is considered an important direction for the next generation of battery technology. Solid-state batteries have higher energy density and longer service life than traditional liquid batteries.

2. Electric motor technology

Electric motor technology is another core technology of new energy vehicles. The electric motor directly affects the driving performance and energy-saving efficiency of the car. Currently, new energy vehicles mainly use two types: permanent magnet synchronous motors and induction motors. Permanent magnet synchronous motor uses rare earth elements to create a permanent magnetic field, which has higher efficiency, high torque and high-power density and smaller size. It also has the characteristics of long service life and easy maintenance. It is one of the most commonly used motor types at present.

Induction motors have the advantages of simple structure and low cost and are widely used in small new energy vehicles. High-efficiency electric motor: This new type of electric motor has higher efficiency and smaller size, further reducing the weight and cost of electric vehicles. In addition, the high-efficiency electric motor also has higher torque output, making electric vehicles smoother when accelerating.

3. Motor Control Technology

The control technology of new energy vehicles includes motor control, battery management, vehicle power control and other aspects. The development of control technology is directly related to the safety, reliability, and performance stability of new energy vehicles. At present, the control technology of new energy vehicles has achieved a high degree of intelligence and automation. For example, the vehicle power control system can automatically adjust the motor power to achieve the best driving effect; the battery management system can monitor the battery status in real time to ensure the safety and safety of the battery.

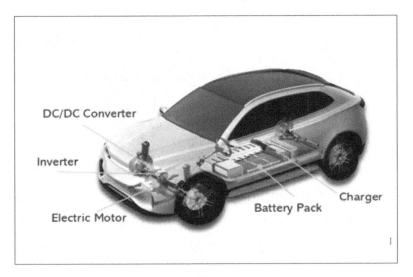

4. Charging technology

The charging technology of new energy vehicles is an important guarantee for their ease of use and charging efficiency. At present, the charging technology of new energy vehicles mainly includes two types: AC charging and DC fast charging. AC charging is suitable for home and commercial charging places, and the charging time is long, generally taking 6 to 8 hours; DC fast charging is suitable for public charging places such as stations and service areas, and the charging speed is fast, and it only takes 20 to 30 minutes to fully charge electricity. In the future, with the popularization of new energy vehicles, the development of charging technology will be more diversified and intelligent, such as the emergence of wireless charging, Internet of Vehicles charging and other technologies.

Wireless charging technology: Solar panels and wireless charging technology is gradually becoming mainstream. It can realize fast charging of electric vehicles through magnetic field induction.

This technology is not only convenient and fast, but also reduces the use of cables and is beneficial to the environment.

Fast charging technology: As the electric vehicle market grows, so does fast charging technology. At present, some electric vehicles can already achieve the goal of being fully charged in 30 minutes.

5. Vehicle electronic technology

Vehicle electronic technology is an important part of new energy vehicles, including vehicle infotainment systems, vehicle navigation systems, vehicle communication systems, etc.

The development of in-vehicle electronics technology has enabled new energy vehicles to achieve a smarter and more convenient driving and travel experience. In the future, with the continuous development of Internet of Vehicles, artificial intelligence and other technologies, the on-board electronic technology of new energy vehicles will also become more intelligent and personalized.

6. Autonomous driving technology

Autonomous driving technology is an important development direction in the field of new energy vehicles. It can not only improve driving safety and comfort, but also reduce the incidence of traffic accidents. At present, many new energy electric vehicles are already equipped with automatic driving assistance systems, such as adaptive cruise control, lane keeping, automatic parking, etc.

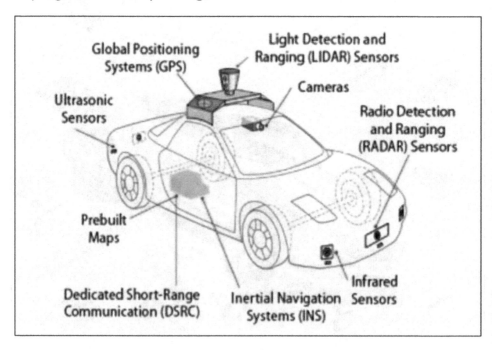

7. Intelligent network technology

Intelligent network technology is an important part of the new energy vehicle field. It can seamlessly connect cars to the Internet and realize information sharing and collaborative control between vehicles. Through intelligent network technology, new energy electric vehicles can achieve remote diagnosis, online upgrades, intelligent navigation, and other functions to improve users' driving experience and convenience.

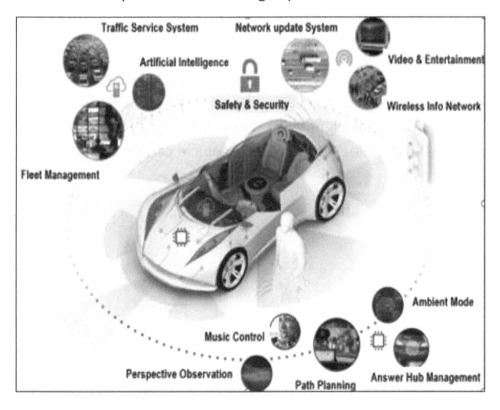

8. Car body material technology

High-strength and lightweight materials: In order to improve the fuel economy and comfort of new energy electric vehicles, body materials are also constantly being upgraded. High-strength lightweight materials such as aluminum alloy and carbon fiber are widely used in the body and chassis components of new energy electric vehicles. These materials not only improve vehicle strength and safety, but also reduce vehicle mass and fuel consumption.

Renewable energy utilization technology: new energy electric vehicles can use roof solar panels or small solar panels installed on the body surface to collect solar energy and store it in batteries for use at night or on rainy days. This renewable energy utilization technology helps reduce vehicle carbon emissions and energy costs.

The electric vehicles' parts and functions

1. Power battery pack

Traction battery packs are also known as electric vehicle batteries (EVB), which powers the electric motor in an electric vehicle. The battery acts as a power storage system, which stores energy in the form of direct current. As the battery kilowatts increase, the range will get higher. Battery life and operation depend on its design, generally traction battery life is estimated at 200,000 miles.

2. Electric motor

An electric motor is a device that drives an electric vehicle. It is an electromagnetic device that converts electrical energy into kinetic energy based on the principle of electromagnetic induction. Its main function is to produce rotational motion that makes the wheel spin.

This is a regenerative braking mechanism, as well as slowing down by converting its kinetic energy into another form and storing it and serving as a power source for electrical equipment or various machines. Basically, there are two types of DC motors and AC motors.

3. DC-DC converter

The traction battery pack provides constant voltage. However, different electric vehicle components have different requirements. The DC-DC converter converts the output power from the distributed battery to the required level. It also provides the voltage needed to charge additional batteries.

4. Power inverter

It converts the battery's DC power into AC power. It also converts the AC current generated during regenerative braking into DC current, which is then used to charge the battery.

5. Charging interface

The charging port connects the electric vehicle to an external power source, to charge the battery. The charging port is sometimes located on the front or back of the electric vehicle.

6. Car charger

Car chargers are used to convert AC power received from the charging port into DC power. The car charger is located and installed in the car, in order to monitor various battery characteristics and control the current flowing in the battery.

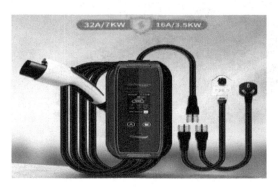

7. Motor control unit

The power electronics controller determines how the electric vehicle works. It regulates electrical energy from the battery to the electric motor. The driver's settings, pedal position determine the speed of the car and the frequency of changes in the input voltage to the motor. It also controls the torque generated.

8. HVAC system

The cooling system usually consists of a radiator, water pump, fan, thermostat, coolant temperature gauge, and drain switch. Electric vehicle engines use two cooling methods, namely air cooling and water cooling. Usually, electric vehicle engines use water cooling. The heating system is provided by electric heaters when necessary.

9. Transmission system

Electric vehicle chassis, because the electric motor has good traction characteristics, the battery vehicle transmission system does not require a clutch and transmission. Vehicle speed control can be achieved with a controller that changes the motor speed through a speed control system. The gearbox transfers mechanical power from the electric motor to the wheels. The advantage of electric vehicles is that they do not require multi-speed transmission, therefore they can avoid power loss, achieving high efficiency.

10. Driving system

The drive system is similar to a fuel-powered vehicle, mainly including the frame, axles, wheels, and suspension. The function of the electric vehicle drive system is to receive torque transmitted from the electric motor through the transmission system, and through adhesion between the drive wheels and the road surface, to produce road surface traction force on the electric vehicle to ensure normal vehicle driving. In addition, as much as possible mitigate the impact and vibration on the vehicle body caused by uneven roads to ensure normal electric vehicle driving.

11. Steering system

The function of the electric vehicle steering system is to maintain or change the driving direction of the electric vehicle. It includes components such as the steering control mechanism, steering gear, and steering transmission mechanism. The steering system consists of the steering wheel, steering gear, steering knuckle, steering knuckle arm, tie rod, straight tie rod, etc. When an electric vehicle turns, it is necessary to ensure a coordinated angular relationship between the steering wheels. The driver controls the steering system to keep the electric vehicle in a straight or turning state, or to change between the above two states of motion; it is also necessary to ensure that the steering wheel does not vibrate, the steering wheel does not swing, and the steering wheel does not vibrate when driving. It is sensitive, has a small minimum rotation diameter and is easy to operate.

12. braking system

Braking system is a general term for all braking and deceleration systems equipped with electric vehicles. Its function is to slow down or stop a moving electric vehicle, or to keep a stopped electric vehicle stationary. The braking system includes brakes and brake transmission devices. Modern electric vehicle braking systems are also equipped with anti-lock braking devices. Similar to fuel vehicles, the braking system of pure electric vehicles also consists of two sets, namely driving brakes and parking brakes.

13. Electrical equipment

Electric vehicle electrical equipment mainly includes batteries, generators, lighting equipment, instruments, audio devices, wipers, etc. The function of the battery is to supply electricity to the starter and electric motor. To meet the needs of high-voltage electric vehicles, electric vehicles usually use a power battery pack formed by several 12V or 24V batteries in series and parallel as their power source. The power battery voltage is 155~400V, which is charged periodically. The electrical energy it stores, as well as its weight and volume, have a decisive impact on the performance of an electric vehicle. Power battery packs take up most of the effective loading space on an electric vehicle and are quite difficult to manage. In general, there are two forms of centralized regulation and decentralized regulation. The Delco battery pack used by General Motors' EV1 adopts a centralized layout, and the support of the power battery pack is a T-shaped frame. The T-shaped frame is installed under the vehicle floor and on the frame under the trunk. The power battery pack is installed on the T-shaped frame and has good stability. It is installed from the rear of the vehicle. The T-shaped frame is equipped with a power battery pack ventilation system, cable protection cover, etc., and automatic and manual circuit breakers are used to cut off the power supply when the vehicle is parked or when the vehicle fails to ensure the safety of the high voltage circuit.

14. Energy recovery system

The function of the energy recovery system is to convert inertial mechanical energy when coasting into electrical energy when the electric vehicle is coasting (or braking) and store it in a capacitor or charge the battery, so that the energy can be immediately released when used.

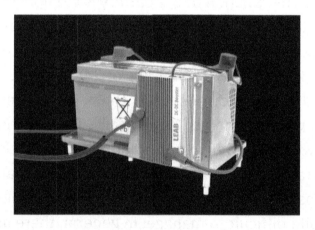

15. Cooling system

Because the battery generates a lot of heat when the vehicle is running, having a good heat dissipation system is crucial for both the safety of the electric vehicle and the life of the battery.

16. Electric car's body

The body is divided into two parts: the front and the compartment. The front of the car can usually accommodate two people, namely the driver and co-driver. The carriages are modified according to customer requirements, including carriage configuration, materials, space design, etc. To maximize passenger comfort, electric vehicles typically use a single-seat side-by-side arrangement, and the number of seats varies depending on the specific model.

17. Industrial devices

Industrial devices are specially designed for industrial electric vehicles to complete work needs, such as lifting equipment, poles, forks, etc. on electric forklifts. Fork lifting and pole tilting are generally done with a hydraulic system driven by an electric motor.

How the Electric Vehicles' work

How do electric cars work? We will introduce in detail the basic principles of electric vehicles, the working principle of electric motors, the advantages of electric vehicles, and the facts drivers should know.

Basic principles of electric vehicles

The basic principle of electric vehicles is to use an electric motor to convert electrical energy into kinetic energy to drive the vehicle. The working principle of electric vehicles is based on magnetism, electric vehicles generate torque through electromagnetic induction to drive wheel movement.

Working principle of electric motor

The electric motor is the core component of an electric vehicle, which converts electrical energy into kinetic energy to drive the vehicle. The working principle of the motor is based on the principle of electromagnetic induction, that is, when current passes through the coil, a magnetic field will be generated around the coil. This magnetic field will interact with the permanent magnet, thereby generating torque and driving the motor to rotate.

Specifically, the electric motor consists of two parts: the stator and the rotor. The stator is composed of a coil and a magnet. When the coil is energized, a magnetic field is generated. The magnet is a permanent magnet, and its magnetic field is fixed. The rotor is composed of a magnet and a shaft. The magnetic field of the magnet interacts with the magnetic field of the stator to generate torque and drive the rotor to rotate.

When the direction of the current changes, the magnetic field of the stator also changes, thereby changing the direction of motion of the rotor.

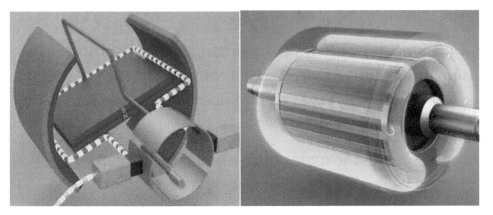

The motor of an electric vehicle can control the speed and steering of the vehicle by controlling the direction and magnitude of the current. Another ingenious thing about electric vehicle power systems is that when the motor rotor is rotated by external energy, it generates electrical energy, and this reversal can charge the vehicle battery. The source of this rotational energy could be a braking car. Therefore, the motor of an electric vehicle can also be charged by recovering braking energy, thereby improving energy efficiency.

Electric vehicles have the following advantages:

Environmental protection and energy saving: Electric vehicles do not require fuel, only electricity, so they do not produce exhaust pollution and are more environmentally friendly. At the same time, electric vehicles are more efficient in energy utilization and can save energy.

High efficiency and low noise: The motor of electric vehicles has high speed and large torque, which can quickly respond to the driver's operation. At the same time, the noise is also very small, making driving more comfortable.

Low maintenance costs: The motor structure of electric vehicles is simple and there are no complex components such as engines and transmissions of traditional vehicles, so maintenance costs are lower.

Energy recovery: The motor of an electric vehicle can be recharged by recovering braking energy, thus extending the actual range of the battery.

Of course, there are challenges and limitations associated with electric vehicles. For example, the driving range and charging time of electric vehicles are still the focus of users, and further development of battery technology can alleviate these problems. In addition, the cost of electric vehicles is still high and needs to be further reduced to become popular.

Step by step the Electric Vehicle works.

Electric vehicles do not require an internal combustion engine to operate, they are powered by an electric motor, not a gasoline-powered engine. The electric motor gets energy from the controller, which regulates the amount of power based on the driver's use of the accelerator pedal. Electric cars use energy stored in rechargeable batteries, which are recharged by ordinary household electricity.

Electric vehicles move along our highways without consuming fuel or producing harmful exhaust emissions while producing less noise pollution. EVs, like automatic cars, have a forward mode and a reverse mode. When you put the vehicle in gear and press the accelerator pedal, this happens, the power is converted from the DC battery to AC for the electric motor, the accelerator pedal sends a signal to the controller, which regulates the vehicle's speed by changing the frequency of the AC power from the inverter to the motor. The motor connects and rotates the wheels through gears. When the brake is applied or the car slows down, the motor becomes an alternator and produces power that is sent back to the battery.

After driving for a certain period of time, the energy in the battery will decrease, so we need to recharge the battery. There are 3 charging speeds for electric vehicles: Slow charging, usually up to 3 kilowatts, often used for charging at night or at work. Charging time takes up to 8 – 10 hours. Fast Changing, typically rated from 7 kilowatts or 22 kilowatts. Usually installed in car parks, supermarkets, leisure centers and homes with off street parking. Charging time takes up to 3 – 4 hours. Rapid charging, typically rated at 43 kilowatts, is only compatible with EVs that have rapid charging capacity. Charging time takes up to 30 – 60 minutes.

The autonomous driving technology

Autonomous driving is a technology that allows vehicles to drive autonomously without human intervention. It uses various sensors, computer vision, artificial intelligence, and machine learning technologies to perceive, analyze and make decisions on the road environment to achieve autonomous navigation and control of vehicles.

The development of autonomous driving technology aims to improve traffic safety, reduce traffic accidents, and provide more efficient traffic flow. It can eliminate traffic accidents caused by factors such as human error, driver fatigue and distraction. In addition, autonomous driving can also improve road utilization, reduce congestion, and reduce energy consumption and emissions.

The fundamentals of autonomous driving

Sensor technology: Autonomous vehicles are usually equipped with a variety of sensors, such as lidar, cameras, radar, and ultrasonic sensors, to sense the surrounding roads and obstacles.

Computer vision: Through image processing and computer vision algorithms, autonomous vehicles can recognize and understand road signs, traffic signals, vehicles, pedestrians, etc.

Perception and positioning: Autonomous vehicles need to sense their own position and surrounding environment in real time in order to make accurate decisions. This can be achieved through the use of technologies such as Global Positioning System (GPS), Inertial Measurement Units (IMU) and map data.

Decision-making and planning: Based on the perceived road and traffic information, autonomous vehicles will use algorithms and models to make decisions and plan appropriate driving paths and actions.

Control system: Autonomous vehicles use control systems to execute the results of decision-making and planning, and control the vehicle's acceleration, braking, steering and other actions.

Currently, autonomous driving technology is in the stage of continuous development and improvement. Several automakers and technology companies have launched partially autonomous vehicles and are testing them on the road. However, the full realization of fully autonomous driving still faces technical, legal, and ethical challenges, and many issues need to be addressed, such as safety, division of responsibilities, and adaptability to road regulations.

The technology of autonomous driving

It is based on advanced sensors, computer vision, artificial intelligence and machine learning technologies, allowing vehicles to perceive the surrounding environment, make decisions and perform corresponding actions.

The following is the general process of autonomous driving technology:

Perception: Autonomous vehicles obtain information such as roads, obstacles, traffic signs and signals through a variety of sensors (such as lidar, cameras, radar, etc.) and convert it into understandable data.

Environment Understanding: Through computer vision and perception algorithms, vehicles analyze and interpret perceived data, identify road signs, vehicles, pedestrians, bicycles, etc., and establish an understanding of the surrounding environment.

Decision Making and Planning: Based on the understanding of the environment, vehicles use algorithms and models to make decisions, such as selecting appropriate lanes, speeds, overtaking actions, etc., and planning the vehicle's driving path.

Control: The control system converts the results of decision-making and planning into vehicle control instructions, including acceleration, braking, steering and other actions to achieve autonomous driving.

The development of autonomous driving technology is gradually achieving the following levels L1-L4:

Assisted driving: Provides some automated functions, such as adaptive cruise control, lane keeping assistance, etc., but still requires human driver monitoring and intervention.

Condition-limited autonomous driving: Under certain conditions, such as on a highway or on a fixed route, the vehicle can drive autonomously but requires a human driver to take over control when needed.

Highly autonomous driving: Vehicles can drive autonomously in most road scenarios, but human drivers still need to be in backup mode in case of emergency.

Fully autonomous driving: The vehicle can drive completely autonomously in various road scenarios without the intervention of a human driver. Achieving this level involves technical, regulatory, and social acceptance challenges.

Autonomous driving technology has the potential to improve traffic safety, increase traffic efficiency and provide travel convenience, but there are still many technical and legal obstacles to overcome.

The autonomous driving projects.

Autonomous driving is an innovative technology designed to enable vehicles to drive and navigate autonomously without human intervention. The goal of this project is to develop autonomous driving systems that can operate safely and efficiently on the road.

Autonomous driving projects utilize advanced sensor technology, artificial intelligence, and machine learning algorithms to enable vehicles to perceive and understand their surrounding environment and make intelligent driving decisions. Project teams typically consist of engineers, data scientists, and automotive experts who work together to design and optimize all aspects of the autonomous driving system.

The main tasks of the project include the following aspects:

Sensor technology: Projects use a variety of sensors to sense the environment around the vehicle, such as radar, lidar, cameras, and ultrasonic sensors. The data collected by these sensors is used to create high-precision maps of the vehicle's surroundings and provide real-time obstacle detection and tracking.

Data processing and perception: Using deep learning and computer vision techniques, the project team processes sensor data and translates it into an understanding of the surrounding environment. This includes identifying and classifying road signs, vehicles, pedestrians, and other obstacles, as well as predicting their behavior and dynamics.

High-precision maps: The project team creates high-precision maps that include information such as road geometry, traffic signs, and traffic signals. These maps provide autonomous driving systems with an important reference needed for navigation and path planning.

Decision-making and planning: Based on the perception of the surrounding environment, the autonomous driving system needs to make decisions and plan the best driving path. This involves following traffic rules, driving safely, choosing routes, and interacting with other vehicles and pedestrians.

Real-time control and execution: The autonomous driving system controls the acceleration, steering and braking of the vehicle based on the planned path and decision-making results. The system needs to constantly monitor and adjust the vehicle's behavior to adapt to changing traffic and road conditions.

The ultimate goal of the autonomous driving project is to achieve fully automated driving, improve traffic safety, reduce traffic congestion, and provide more efficient and convenient travel methods. Although autonomous driving technology has achieved some success in different test environments, it is still difficult to achieve widespread commercial application.

The self-driving cars

Autonomous Driving Cars refer to automotive systems that can drive and operate independently without the direct control of a human driver. This kind of car uses advanced technologies such as various sensors, computer vision technology, artificial intelligence, and machine learning algorithms to be able to sense and understand the surrounding environment and make corresponding decisions and actions.

The goals of autonomous vehicles are to increase road safety, improve traffic efficiency, reduce traffic congestion, and provide passengers with a more comfortable and convenient travel experience. They can autonomously choose the optimal route through pre-set destinations and comply with traffic rules, while adapting to various complex traffic environments and road conditions.

To achieve autonomous driving, cars are equipped with a variety of sensors such as lidar, cameras, radar, and ultrasonic sensors to obtain data on the surrounding environment. These sensors transmit data to the computer system on the vehicle, which analyzes and processes the data to identify roads, obstacles, traffic signs and other vehicles.

Based on these sensory data, self-driving cars use artificial intelligence and machine learning algorithms to analyze road conditions and make decisions, such as accelerating, decelerating, turning, and changing lanes. They can adjust accordingly to real-time changes in the surrounding environment to ensure safe and efficient driving.

Current autonomous driving technology is constantly evolving and improving. Some automakers and technology companies are already conducting tests and pilot projects of self-driving cars on actual roads. However, there are many technical, regulatory, and ethical challenges that need to be addressed to achieve fully autonomous vehicles. It is expected that in the next few years, as the technology further matures, and regulations are gradually improved, autonomous vehicles will gradually enter the stage of commercial application.

The autonomous driving industry

The autonomous driving industry refers to the industrial field involving autonomous driving technology, related equipment, and services. It includes participants from all aspects, including automakers, technology companies, suppliers, research institutions, and government regulators.

The autonomous driving industry has developed rapidly in the past few years and attracted a lot of investment and attention. Here are a few important aspects of the industry:

Automobile manufacturers: Many traditional automobile manufacturers are actively investing in the field of autonomous driving, developing, and launching their own brands of autonomous vehicles. At the same time, some emerging automakers have also joined the competition and launched electric vehicles with self-driving capabilities.

Technology companies: Many well-known technology companies have also made significant investments and R&D efforts in the field of autonomous driving.

These companies include Google's subsidiary Waymo, Tesla, Apple, Amazon, Huawei, Baidu, BYD etc. They use advanced technologies such as artificial intelligence, machine learning, sensor technology and map data in the field of autonomous driving.

Suppliers: Self-driving cars require a vast array of sensors, computer hardware, software systems and other components. Suppliers play an important role in the industry, providing critical technology and equipment to support the development and production of autonomous vehicles.

Research institutions: Many universities and research institutions are dedicated to research and innovation in autonomous driving technology. They conduct various experiments and trials, promote the continuous progress of autonomous driving technology, and provide relevant academic support.

Government regulators: The autonomous driving industry faces many challenges, including issues with regulations and safety standards. Government regulators will need to develop policies and regulations to ensure the safety and compliance of autonomous vehicles.

The autonomous driving industry has bright prospects and is expected to continue to grow in the coming years. As technology further matures and regulations are gradually improved, autonomous vehicles will gradually become mainstream and have a profound impact on transportation, urban planning, and travel patterns.

The autonomous driving chips.

Autonomous driving chips are one of the key technologies used to realize autonomous driving functions. It is an integrated circuit chip that is embedded in a vehicle to provide the vehicle with sensing, decision-making and control capabilities, allowing it to drive autonomously on the road.

Autonomous driving chips usually consist of multiple functional modules, including perception modules, decision-making modules, and execution modules.

The perception module is responsible for sensing information about the environment around the vehicle. It uses various sensor technologies such as lidar, cameras, radar, and ultrasonic sensors to obtain data on roads, vehicles, pedestrians, and other obstacles. This data is transmitted to the autonomous driving chip for processing and analysis.

The decision-making module uses the data provided by the perception module, combined with the vehicle's internal map, navigation system and preset driving strategy, to make corresponding decisions. It can determine the vehicle's driving path, speed and control method based on road conditions, traffic rules and dynamic information from other vehicles.

The execution module is responsible for converting the instructions generated by the decision-making module into actual vehicle actions. It is connected to the vehicle's control system and can control the vehicle's steering, acceleration, braking and other operations to achieve automatic driving functions.

Autonomous driving chips usually require powerful computing power and a high degree of real-time performance to process large amounts of sensory data and complex decision-making algorithms. Therefore, modern autonomous driving chips usually use high-performance processors, graphics processing units (GPUs), and artificial intelligence accelerators to meet these requirements.

The development of autonomous driving chips is of great significance to the commercialization and popularization of autonomous driving technology. It can improve driving safety, efficiency, and comfort, and provide solutions to problems such as traffic congestion, energy consumption and environmental protection. As technology continues to develop, it is expected that autonomous driving chips will continue to evolve to achieve more intelligent and reliable autonomous driving systems.

The autonomous driving algorithms

The automatic driving algorithm is the core part of realizing the automatic driving function. It uses sensor data and vehicle internal information to control the driving of the vehicle through perception and decision-making of the environment.

Here are some common self-driving algorithms:

Perception Algorithms: Perception algorithms are used to extract information about the vehicle's surroundings from sensor data. These algorithms can process different types of data such as lidar, cameras, radar, and ultrasonic sensors, and perform tasks such as obstacle detection, lane detection, traffic signal detection, etc. Common perception algorithms include point cloud processing, target detection, image recognition, and sensor fusion.

Positioning and mapping algorithms: Positioning and mapping algorithms are used to determine the position and attitude of the vehicle on the map. These algorithms use information such as Global Positioning System (GPS), Inertial Measurement Unit (IMU), visual odometry and map data to accurately position and build environmental maps to help vehicles accurately perceive and understand the surrounding environment.

Path Planning Algorithm: The path planning algorithm determines the path of the vehicle on the road. It considers factors such as the vehicle's current location, target location, road information, and traffic rules to generate a safe and efficient driving path. These algorithms can use techniques such as heuristic search, planning graph search, and genetic algorithms to find the best path in complex environments.

Decision-making and control algorithm: The decision-making and control algorithm makes decisions and controls the vehicle's actions based on the results of perception and path planning. It can determine the vehicle's speed, steering and braking operations based on information such as road conditions, traffic signals, and obstacles ahead. These algorithms are usually implemented using methods such as model predictive control, proportional–integral–derivative (PID) control, and state machines.

Artificial intelligence and machine learning algorithms: Artificial intelligence and machine learning algorithms are widely used in the field of autonomous driving. They can be used in various aspects such as perception, decision-making and control. For example, deep learning algorithms can be used for target detection and image recognition, and reinforcement learning algorithms can be used to learn vehicle behavior strategies and optimize path planning.

These algorithms are often used in combination to form a complete autonomous driving system. Different autonomous driving algorithms can be adjusted and optimized according to specific needs and scenarios to improve the performance of the autonomous driving system.

The autonomous driving data sets

Autonomous driving data sets refer to large-scale data sets used to train and evaluate autonomous driving systems. These datasets typically contain data acquired by various sensors (such as cameras, lidar, radar, etc.), as well as label or annotation information associated with these sensors.

The purpose of the autonomous driving data set is to provide enough samples for the machine learning algorithm so that it can understand and interpret the road environment, traffic signs, vehicle behavior, etc., and make corresponding decisions. The construction of these datasets often involves collecting large amounts of sensor data in real road environments and labeling or annotating the data by manual or semi-automatic means.

Autonomous driving datasets typically contain the following types of data:

Image data: A sequence of continuous images captured by a camera, used to identify, and understand road environments, traffic signs, pedestrians, vehicles, etc.

Point cloud data: Point cloud data generated by lidar scanning is used to build a three-dimensional model of the surrounding environment.

Situational data: environmental data obtained by vehicle sensors, such as vehicle status, GPS location, vehicle speed, etc.

Label or annotation data: Label or annotation information associated with sensor data, such as object detection boxes, semantic segmentation masks, behavioral labels, etc.

The size of autonomous driving data sets is usually large to ensure that machine learning algorithms can achieve good performance in various complex road scenarios. These datasets play a vital role in developing and testing autonomous driving systems and provide researchers and developers with baseline data to improve algorithms and evaluate system performance.

It is worth noting that due to the continuous development and technological advancement in the field of autonomous driving, autonomous driving data sets may contain different types and qualities of data and will be continuously updated and evolved to reflect the latest challenges and needs.

Some common autonomous driving data sets

KITTI dataset: The KITTI dataset is a widely used autonomous driving dataset that provides various sensor data from real road environments, including camera images, lidar data, inertial measurement unit (IMU) data, etc. It contains a large amount of annotation data, such as target detection boxes, semantic segmentation labels, optical flow estimation, etc., and can be used to train and evaluate various autonomous driving tasks.

Cityscapes dataset: The Cityscapes dataset focuses on urban scenes and provides a large collection of high-resolution camera images and semantic segmentation labels. This data set contains complex scenes such as various urban roads, traffic signs, pedestrians, and vehicles, and is suitable for perception and understanding tasks in autonomous driving.

ApolloScape data set: ApolloScape is an autonomous driving data set provided by Baidu, which contains rich sensor data, such as camera images, lidar data, radar data, etc. The data set covers a variety of road scenes and provides various label information, such as vehicle detection boxes, lane line annotations, etc.

nuScenes dataset: The nuScenes dataset provides sensor data from real urban environments, including camera images, lidar data, radar data, etc. Scenes in the data set include city streets, highways, etc., as well as various complex traffic scenes and weather conditions.

Udacity Autonomous Driving Dataset: Udacity provides an open autonomous driving dataset that contains sensor data collected on real roads. This data set is widely used for education and research on autonomous driving algorithms, including image classification, target detection, lane line detection and other tasks.

These datasets represent only a small fraction of those available in the field of autonomous driving. As technology develops and research advances, more data sets will emerge to meet the needs of different scenarios and tasks.

The autonomous vehicle control modules

The autonomous vehicle control module is one of the core components in the autonomous driving system. It is responsible for controlling the driving and maneuvering of the vehicle based on perception and decision-making results. Autonomous vehicle control modules usually include the following sub-modules:

Vehicle status monitoring: This module is used to monitor and measure the status of the vehicle, including vehicle speed, acceleration, steering angle, braking status, etc. It can obtain this information through sensor data, vehicle bus systems and other sensor interfaces.

Path planning: The path planning module uses the vehicle's current location, target location, and map data to calculate the best path the vehicle should travel. It considers factors such as road restrictions, traffic regulations, speed limits and environmental obstacles to generate a safe and efficient driving path.

Vehicle control: The vehicle control module converts instructions generated by path planning into specific vehicle actions to control vehicle acceleration, braking, steering and other operations. This is typically accomplished by communicating with the vehicle's electronic control unit (ECU) or control system.

Dynamic obstacle sensing and tracking: This module is responsible for sensing and tracking dynamic obstacles around the vehicle, such as other vehicles, pedestrians, and bicycles. It uses sensor data, such as radar, cameras and lidar, to detect the location, speed and trajectory of obstacles and provides this information to path planning and vehicle control modules to avoid collisions while driving.

Lane Keeping and Assistance System: This module is used to keep the vehicle in the correct lane and provide driving assistance functions such as adaptive cruise control (ACC) and lane departure warning. It uses lane line detection and lane keeping algorithms, combined with the vehicle control module, to enable the vehicle to maintain stable driving within the lane.

These modules will work together through data interaction and control instruction transmission to achieve safe and efficient driving of autonomous vehicles. These modules typically use high-performance processors and algorithms to handle real-time perception and decision-making tasks and are tightly integrated with the vehicle's hardware systems. With the development of autonomous driving technology, control modules are constantly optimized and innovated to achieve higher.

EV Battery Manufacturing Industry

Batteries are an important part of Electric Vehicles, which account for about 30% of the total production costs of an EV. In 2023, total global lithium battery shipments will reach 1,300 GWh, a year-on-year increase of 35.7%. Lithium-ion battery shipments in China will reach 749.0 GWh in 2023, a year-on-year increase of 44.6%, accounting for 57.6% of the world's total lithium-ion battery shipments. The Market Research Company estimates that in 2025 and 2030, global lithium-ion battery shipments will reach 2,211.8 GWh and 6,080.4 GWh respectively, with a compound growth rate of 22.8%.

Top 10 Global power battery manufacturers in 2023 (1-11)

Rank	Manufacturer	Installed Capacity (GWh)	yearly Increased	Market share (%)
1	CATL	233.4	48.3 %	37.4 %
2	BYD	98.3	60.4 %	15.7 %
3	LG New Energy	84.8	41.8 %	13.6 %
4	Panasonic	40.3	27.5 %	6.5 %
5	SK Innovation	30.9	13.5 %	5.0 %
6	Zhongxin	29.1	74.1 %	4.7 %
7	Samsung SDI	28.2	38.4 %	4.5 %
8	Guoxuan HT	14.9	18.5 %	2.4 %
9	Yiwei Energy	13.4	131.9 %	2.1 %
10	Funeng Tech	8.9	41.7 %	1.4 %

Source: SNE Research

From January to November 2023, the global installed capacity of new energy vehicles (EV, PHEV, HEV) batteries was approximately 624.4GWh, an increase of 41.8% over the same period in 2022. Judging from the top ten companies in terms of global power battery installed capacity from January to November 2023, Chinese companies still occupy six seats, namely CATL, BYD, Zhongxin, Guoxuan Hi-Tech, Yiwei Lithium Energy, and Funeng Technology, which occupying 63.7 % of market share. South Korea 23.1 % and Japan 6.5%. Total of 93.3 % global market share.

In 2023, January to November, the power battery is installed by the companies as follow:

Power battery installed by companies

Rank	Manufacturer	Installed Capacity (GWh)	Mainly by company
1	CATL	233.4	Tesla, Volkswagen, Volvo, BMW, Chery, GAC-Aian, Geely, etc.
2	BYD	98.3	BYD
3	LG New Energy	84.8	Tesla, Volkswagen, Toyota, GM, Honda, Nissan, BMW, Ford, etc.
4	Panasonic	40.3	Tesla
5	SK Innovation	30.9	Mercedes Benz, Modern Group, Volkswagen, Ford, etc.
6	Zhongxin	29.1	GAC-Aian, Xiaopeng, Chang'an, Li Auto, etc.
7	Samsung SDI	28.2	Volkswagen, BMW, Ford, GM, Volvo, Stellantis.
8	Guoxuan HT	14.9	Saic-GM-Wuling, Geely, Chang'an Great Wall, etc.
9	Yiwei Energy	13.4	GAC-Aian, Xiaopeng, Chang'an, Hezhong NE, Brilliance-BMB, etc.
10	Funeng Tech	8.9	Mercedes-Benz, GAC-Aian, Lantu Auto, Skyworth Auto, etc.

Source: Writer Analysis

Tesla (USA) mainly uses batteries from Japan and South Korea, while Tesla (Shanghai) uses batteries from CATL. Most German car manufacturers use batteries made in China. Some Chinese automakers also produce power batteries for themselves.

Currently, there are four main types of power batteries on the market: lead-acid batteries, nickel-based batteries, lithium-ion batteries and fuel cells. Their respective characteristics are as follows:

Lead-acid batteries are one of the earliest applied power batteries. They have the advantages of low cost, high safety, and good high-current discharge performance. However, they also have shortcomings such as low specific energy, heavy weight, and non-environmental protection. Lead-acid batteries are mainly used in low-speed electric vehicles, electric bicycles and backup power supplies.

Nickel-based batteries include nickel-cadmium batteries, nickel-zinc batteries and nickel-metal hydride batteries. They have the advantages of long cycle life, high charge and discharge efficiency, and good over-discharge resistance. However, they also have low specific energy, obvious memory effects, and contain toxic metals and other shortcomings. Nickel-based batteries are mainly used in hybrid vehicles and some small pure electric vehicles.

Lithium-ion batteries are one of the most mainstream power batteries at present. It has the advantages of high specific energy, small size, light weight, small self-discharge, and no memory effect. However, it also has shortcomings such as poor safety, high cost, and short cycle life. Lithium-ion batteries are mainly used in pure electric vehicles and some hybrid vehicles.

A fuel cell is a device that directly converts chemical energy into electrical energy. It has the advantages of high energy conversion efficiency, no environmental pollution, and only water as its product. However, it also has the disadvantages of high technical difficulty, high cost, and complex hydrogen storage problems. Fuel cells are mainly used in buses, trucks and special purpose vehicles.

With the advancement of science and technology and market demand, various types of power batteries are constantly undergoing technological innovation and industrial upgrading to improve performance, reduce costs and ensure safety. In the future, power batteries will play an important role in more fields and provide reliable energy for green travel.

Some improvement idea

1. New energy vehicles, sometimes charging the battery is difficult and time consuming. By changing the battery storage compartment in such a way, the battery is made into several parts, so it is easy to remove and exchange for a new battery. When you come to a battery charging station, just swap it, calculate the energy used, pay and you're done.

2. After achieving wireless charging, the next step is to install charging on the road, where the stop lights are installed. When the car stops, battery charging takes place, the next time the car starts, charging stops. Charging fees can be calculated how long it takes.

3. New energy vehicles appear on the roads, highways, parking lots, and are exposed to sunlight. So, how do you use solar energy as a power source to drive a car, by using the entire body as a solar panel? This is a new technology worth thinking about.

4. Regarding property rights, in new energy vehicles, there are thousands of chips, which have various functions. Through collaboration between research institutions, companies and the government, determining standards and patenting the results of these creations. So that it can be used together with paying for patent rights. Isn't it better than being controlled by each company, sometimes benefiting another company without paying anything?

Introduction to CATL

Contemporary Amperex Technology Co. Limited (abbreviated as **CATL**) was founded in Ningde City, Fujian Province, China. It is a battery manufacturer and technology company founded in 2011 that specializes in the manufacturing of lithium-ion batteries for electric vehicles and energy storage systems, as well as battery management systems (BMS).

The company started as a Amperex Technology Limited (ATL), a previous business founded by Robin Zeng in 1999. ATL initially manufactured lithium-polymer batteries based on licensed technology, but later developed more reliable battery designs themselves. In 2005 ATL was acquired by Japan's TDK company, but Robin Zeng continued as a manager. In 2012, Robin Zeng and vice-chairman Huang Shilin spun-off the EV battery operations of ATL into the new company CATL, with local government own 40% stake of the company. Until 2015, former parent TDK held a 15% stake in CATL.

CATL from zero to the biggest in the world in ten years

After graduation in 1985, Robin Zeng went to Guangdong and joined Xinke Magnetic Power Plant, a foreign-owned enterprise in Dongguan. Because of his outstanding abilities, he was quickly recognized by his boss and was promoted to management soon after. Later, he was sent abroad by the company for further study to learn battery production technology.

At the age of 31, Robin Zeng became the youngest engineering director and the first mainland director. However, Robin Zeng's heart was not here. Because it is a foreign-funded enterprise,

Robin Zeng's position can be said to be the ceiling, and even if he is the director, his voice in the company is very limited.

Start with a mobile phone battery!

At that time, the company's CEO Liang Shaokang felt that with the rise of mobile phones, the future potential of the battery market was huge, and he wanted to invite Robin Zeng to start a business together. He also invited the old leader Chen Tanghua to serve as a lobbyist. Hearing that the two leaders were full of unlimited expectations for the future battery market, Robin Zeng was moved this time.

In 1999, three people established ATL together and established the first factory in Dongguan. When they first started their business, Robin Zeng and others chose to disassemble the batteries in Nokia for research. After comparison, a small and thin polymer lithium battery was finally selected.

For this battery patent, Robin Zeng flew to the United States and went to Bell Labs to spend a huge amount of money to buy it. But things didn't go so smoothly. At that time, more than 20 companies across the country purchased this patent, but no one discovered that this patent had a very serious problem: the battery would inflate and deform after being charged multiple times.

But the United States says this is unavoidable. In order to solve this problem, Robin Zeng locked himself in the research and development room, tried dozens of electrolyte formulas, and devoted himself to solving the battery bulge problem. After several weeks, he finally found the source of the problem: the wrong composition of the electrolyte. After repeated modifications, Robin Zeng finally made a finished battery that is airtight and became the first company to successfully use this technology.

The success of this technology made Robin Zeng's company famous in the industry. Not only are they half the price of Korean batteries, they also have double the capacity. Although big companies such as Nokia and Motorola still haven't chosen Robin Zeng's batteries, many bulk mobile phone companies have chosen him.

At this time, the domestic battery market situation was just as Liang Shaokang expected: the rapid growth of the mobile phone market has driven batteries. In 2003, Robin Zeng's company developed a new polymer lithium battery and obtained batteries for Apple's 18 million iPods. Later, ATL also helped Apple solve the problem of short cycle life of MP3 lithium batteries and became Samsung's first choice after the "Samsung Explosion Gate" incident.

These achievements laid a solid foundation for his future business credibility. In 2008, at the Olympic Games in China to promote new energy vehicles, Robin Zeng is keenly aware that this is a new trend and at this time, the country restricts the production of power batteries by foreign-funded enterprises. This is an excellent opportunity for local enterprises.

Enter new energy vehicle batteries!

In 2011, Robin Zeng founded CATL in Ningde City. When Robin Zeng first established CATL, BYD Wang Chuanfu was already the leader in the domestic power battery field. Wang Chuanfu enjoys the title of entrepreneur "technical madman", but 10 years later, he was left behind by this rising star. How did Robin Zeng do it when he was inferior in financial experience and other aspects? This is mainly due to their different strategic visions.

At that time, there were two main technical routes for developing car batteries. One is a lithium iron phosphate battery, which has low cost and high stability, but has poor battery life. The other type is ternary lithium battery, which is expensive and has poor stability, but has strong battery life. Robin Zeng aimed at the second route. He said firmly: What is the biggest problem that consumers worry about when buying electric cars is the poor charging range. For this reason, he spared no effort to develop ternary lithium batteries, while Wang Chuanfu chose iron phosphate lithium batteries.

However, the cost of ternary lithium is too high, accounting for more than 30% of the total cost of a car. Although the early development was relatively smooth, compared with the capital costs of research and development, it can only be supported with difficulty. In the case of high cost, almost most of the automotive battery industry chooses lithium iron phosphate batteries.

Under the pressure of the market and capital, Robin Zeng still firmly believes that high battery life is the future trend. Why did Robin Zeng choose ternary lithium so firmly? It turns out that in 2012, China issued a new energy development plan, and Robin Zeng believed that the country would support new energy. As expected, three years later, the state began to implement subsidies for new energy vehicles. Subsidies for battery companies are calculated based on cruising range. This undoubtedly makes Robin Zeng, who developed ternary lithium batteries, the biggest beneficiary.

Technological breakthroughs and market expansion: CATL has been committed to the research, development, and innovation of lithium-ion battery technology since its establishment. They made important breakthroughs in battery energy density, safety, and lifespan, and began to promote their products to domestic and foreign markets.

Cooperation with partners: CATL has established cooperative relationships with a number of internationally renowned automobile manufacturers to provide them with battery products and solutions. These partners include BMW, Volkswagen, Toyota, Chery, etc. These partnerships provide CATL with broader market opportunities and accelerate the company's development.

Under state subsidies, the selling price of new energy vehicles is even cheaper than ordinary cars. The new energy vehicle market is also growing at a rate of doubling every year, and many consumers are choosing ternary lithium batteries with longer battery life. Hyundai, Jaguar, Land Rover, and many other brands have chosen to cooperate with CATL. Whose has surpassed BYD and become the number one in the industry.

It only took Robin Zeng seven years from the establishment of CATL to become the world's king of lithium batteries. The per capita salary of CATL employees in 2017 was as high as 250,000 yuan, ranking first in the industry, and it was still in the third-tier city of Ningde. In Ningde City, with the help of Robin Zeng Enterprises, GDP has grown at a rapid rate of 30% in just a few years. Many Ningde people, when they mention Robin Zeng and CATL, their eyes show admiration and pride.

But Robin Zeng, the glorious leader, knew very well that in the prosperous age, there were great hidden dangers. State subsidies will one day be cancelled, (terminated in 2022) and foreign-funded companies will always come in. When all of this comes, will CATL still be like what it is now? This is the hidden danger that Robin Zeng is worried about.

To this end, he spent money to buy mines around the world, because China's lithium resource reserves only account for 6% of the world's lithium resources, and 80% rely on imports. Robin Zeng did this in order to reduce battery costs. Competing for talents is always one of the core competitiveness of an enterprise. Robin Zeng takes this very seriously and spends a lot of money to recruit talents. He holds nearly half of the people with doctorates in the lithium battery industry in the country.

Sure enough, in June 2019, after the "Typhoon" left, the Ministry of Industry and Information Technology abolished the "Automotive Power Battery Industry Specifications", and a large number of foreign companies such as Samsung and Panasonic rushed in. Opportunities are always reserved for those who are prepared. This saying is still relevant today. This even crazier new energy battery competition did not dislodge CATL, but it actually gained the upper hand.

Looking at the domestic market share, CATL has risen from 12.23% in 2015 to 52.14% in 2019. A big reason for this is that Robin Zeng took precautions and made all preparations when he was protected by national policies. Even Tesla announced in January 2020 that "we have cooperated with CATL, China's largest new energy vehicle battery supplier."

By this year, new energy vehicles have ushered in an explosive period again, and many new energy vehicle stocks have experienced skyrocketing gains, especially Tesla. As Tesla's best partner, Robin Zeng of CATL was nicknamed "the man behind Musk."

In ten years, CATL has grown from a few factories to a leading battery company, which is inseparable from Robin Zeng's accurate control of the overall situation. His strong entrepreneurial spirit turned into infinite wisdom, flowing endlessly like spring water. However, the Chinese market has never lacked competitors. Let us wait and see whether Robin Zeng can continue to maintain his position as a leading company in the future!

Introduction to BYD

Build **Y**our **D**ream was founded by Wang Chuan-Fu in 1995, doing business in the battery and mobile phone batteries. It started manufacturing cars in 2002. In March 2022, when it announced the discontinuation of fuel vehicles, its market value exceeded one trillion yuan for the first time in June. In August, it entered the Fortune 500 list globally. There are 23 automakers in total, 7 of which are from China. Among these 7 automakers, BYD is the only one that focuses on the production of new energy vehicles. The three major businesses are new energy vehicles and related businesses, electronics sub-rechargeable batteries and photovoltaic power generation business. The core strengths of vertical integration and leading technology make BYD extremely competitive. Its blade battery, DM-i super hybrid e-platform 3.0, CTB battery body integration, iTA intelligent transportation and smart city. The main business of BYD Electronics is mostly semiconductor foundry business. The mainstream mobile phone brands in the market, such as: Huawei, Xiaomi, Samsung, Honor, OPPO, etc., have foundry cooperation with BYD Electronics, it also manufactures all automotive-grade chips for new energy vehicles. In China, more than half of the history of mobile communication development has been witnessed and participated by BYD Electronics. BYD Auto's business covers seven conventional fields, including public transport taxis, private cars, buses, urban commodity logistics, urban building logistics, and sanitation. At the same time, it has also launched a variety of electric special vehicles for major special fields, such as: airports, seaports, mines, and warehousing. According to BYD's planning and setting in the rail transit solution, the sky rail with medium traffic volume and the sky shuttle bus with low traffic volume are proposed, which is also based on its own integrated innovation advantages and extends the electric vehicle industry chain. Simply put, it is BYD's Sky Rail Transportation and shuttle are the cross-border integration of BYD's new energy vehicle bus and rail transit technology. It combines the natural advantages of electrification and intelligence, and greatly reduces construction and operation costs, which is about 15% to 20% of the subway, about one-third. One of the construction cycles is very suitable for the changes in urban traffic in the future. In the Research and Development department, BYD's R&D expenditure has reached 18.654 billion yuan in 2022, meanwhile it will reach 20 billion yuan in 2023. By the end of 2022, the total number of BYD employees reached 650,000, and will reach 900,000 by the end of 2023, with an average salary of 107,300 yuan per year. In the new energy vehicles, BYD is currently building 9 factories in China, one in Thailand and one in Vietnam, with total capacities 6 million vehicles. Recently, BYD announced the establishment of three new energy comprehensive factories in Brazil, one factory for electric buses and truck chassis, a new energy passenger vehicle production factory, and a processing factory specializing in lithium iron phosphate battery materials.

Among them, a new energy passenger vehicle production line, covering pure electric and plug-in hybrid models. The planned annual production capacity will reach 150,000 vehicles, with an investment of 4.5 billion yuan, and it will be put into operation in the second half of 2024, which is expected to create more than 5,000 local jobs. Overall, for the first 6 months of 2023 BYD has sold 1,25 million vehicles and at the end of 2023, it is expected to sell 3.0 million vehicles. Nowadays, new energy vehicles are not only for transportation, but loaded with technology, intelligence, and conveniences.

BYD has expanded its sales overseas, to European countries, Scandinavia, Southeast Asian countries, Australia, Middle Eastern countries, Latin American countries, and African countries, sales to more than 55 countries worldwide. Due to high transportation costs and limited capacities available for car exports. Recently BYD acquired a ro-ro ship capable of transporting 7000 vehicles and ordered 8 ro-ro ships. This marked the official formation of its maritime shipping fleet. In 2024, exports are expected to exceed 600,000 vehicles, after experiencing a surge in domestic sales, BYD has expanded its presence in overseas markets and has entered several countries and regions in Asia, Europe, the Middle East, Africa, North America, and South America.

Made in the USA
Las Vegas, NV
26 January 2024

84908783R00050